Things I Ponder

by Sandy McClure

illustrations by
Sherry A. Mitcham

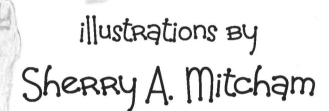

XULON PRESS

MW00885104

for
Emma Grace

for
Bill & Chloe

Sandy McClure

Copyright © 2011 by Sandy McClure

Things I Ponder
by Sandy McClure

Printed in the United States of America

ISBN 9781619040472

www.xulonpress.com

Sometimes I lie awake at night,
pondering the great mysteries of life ...

... like why Do cats chase their tails?

And who is faster ... turtles? ... snails?

How Do stars know when to come out?
Why are there too many to count?

Where Does the sun go at night to hide?
Before it sneaks up the other side?

Why Do geese fly in V's?
So the ones in back can feel the breeze?

How Does the Earth know what to grow?
How Do plants stay safe in snow?

How do the waves know where to stop?

Why is rain shaped like a drop?

Why Do we close our eyes when we sneeze?

Why are Dogs a home for fleas?

These things I ponder in my bed ...

... so many questions in my head!

Where Do Dolphins sleep at night?

Why Do fireflies need a light?

How do birds know what to sing?
And where to fly every spring?

Why Does pollen make me sneeze?
But never seems to bother bees?

Why is my shadow sometimes tall?

... and other times it's very small?

How Does the Earth know what I need?
To help me grow just like the seeds?

I asked my Mimi about these things.
She said, "God is our omnipotent King!"

"That word means God made all that is ...
the earth ... the stars ... <u>YOU</u> ... are His!
Animals ... plants ... the ground you trod ...
... it all sprang from the Word of God!"

"He did not leave anything out,
or fret or toss or turn about.
Not only that, He guides us, too.
<u>L</u>et's honor Him in all we do."

Thank you, God, for loving me,
and making all these things I see.

Good night, Mimi. Good night, God ...
... my sleepy head begins to nod ...

One more thing I want to know ...
...just one more thing before you go ...
... how long does it take giraffes to swallow?
Mimi says ...

"Let's ponder that ..."

... tomorrow!"

Sandy McClure has lived in Georgia all her life,
with the exception of a year in South Africa.
She is a certified Language Arts teacher,
a Sunday School teacher, and a former business owner.
She recently collaborated with her sisters to
write a children's epic, *The Chipmunk Family Odyssey*.
She is a proud mother to Lauren and grandmother to Emma Grace.
She lives with her husband, Bill, in Powder Springs, Georgia.

Sherry Mitcham is a native Atlantan
now living in Fayetteville, Georgia
with her husband, Bill, and her cockerpoo, Chloe.
She is a professional graphic artist and a
self-taught colored pencil artist.
Things I Ponder is her first published children's book ...
she hopes to do many, many more!